Poems From Scotland

Edited By Kelly Scannell

First published in Great Britain in 2019 by:

Young Writers
Remus House
Coltsfoot Drive
Peterborough
PE2 9BF
Telephone: 01733 890066
Website: www.youngwriters.co.uk

All Rights Reserved
Book Design by Ashley Janson
© Copyright Contributors 2018
SB ISBN 978-1-78988-068-7
Printed and bound in the UK by BookPrintingUK
Website: www.bookprintinguk.com
YB0386K

FOREWORD

Here at Young Writers, we love to let imaginations run wild and creativity go crazy. Our aim is to encourage young people to get their creative juices flowing and put pen to paper. Each competition is tailored to the relevant age group, hopefully giving each pupil the inspiration and incentive to create their own piece of creative writing, whether it's a poem or a short story. By allowing them to see their own work in print, we know their confidence and love for the written word will grow.

For our latest competition Poetry Wonderland, we invited primary school pupils to create wild and wonderful poems on any topic they liked – the only limits were the limits of their imagination! Using poetry as their magic wand, these young poets have conjured up worlds, creatures and situations that will amaze and astound or scare and startle! Using a variety of poetic forms of their own choosing, they have allowed us to get a glimpse into their vivid imaginations. We hope you enjoy wandering through the wonders of this book as much as we have.

CONTENTS

Carmuirs Primary School, Camelon

Zach Finlayson (8)	61
Tiegan McLaughlan (9)	62
Aleisha Brown (10)	63
Claudia Scobbie (9)	64
Roxanne Jones (9)	65
Cody Clark (9)	66
Arran Frederick (8)	67
Ryan Walsh (9)	68
Owen Sommerville (9)	69

Cults Primary School, Cults

Erin Harnett (8)	70
Artemy Melgui (9)	71
Ava Skinner (9)	72
James Street (9)	73
Wajeeha Hamid (9)	74
Fatema Gomaa (9)	75
Ben Smart (9)	76
Yaseen Zweit (9)	77
Keanna Couch (9)	78
Hollie Chalmers (8)	79
Lucy MacDonald (9)	80
Taha Zweit (9)	81
Gavin Pedrog (9)	82
Sienna Herd (8)	83
Nika Sharifi (8)	84

Echline Primary School, South Queensferry

Adam Balanowski (9)	85
Olivia Ferguson (9)	86
Isobel Buckley (9)	87
Shay Alexander Hand (9)	88
Jack Crow (9)	89
Caleb Munro (9)	90
Katie Hughes (9)	91
Connell Walker (9)	92

Falla Hill Primary School, Fauldhouse

Rebecca Murtagh (11)	93
Sean McDonald (11)	94
Sarah McLean Abbott (11)	96
Charlie Bruce Allen (10)	98
Alexander Cook (10)	100
Amber Gourlay (10)	102
Leah Brand (10)	104
Dylan Rae (10)	105
Adrian Macrae (11)	106
Thomas Charles William Swan (11)	107
Grace Blair (10)	108
Sophie Robertson (11)	109
Elle Wightman (10)	110
Abigail Mclernon (10)	111
Maci Carty (10)	112
Max Macfarlane (11)	113
Lauren McMillan (10)	114
Caitlin Donnelly (11)	115
Cameron Mullen (9)	116
Mark Reilly (10)	117
James Walker (9)	118
Kirsten Law (10)	119
Chloe Cunningham (10)	120
Leona Lawrence (11)	121
Riley Burns (9)	122
Kelsey Mcdougall (10)	123

High Mill Primary School, Carluke

Samantha Murray (11)	124
Matthew Russell (10)	125
Sarah Madill (9)	126
Jasmin Peebles (10)	127
Oliver Isik (10)	128
Dominic Dickson (10)	129
Chelsea Gault (11)	130

Riverbank School, Aberdeen

Bethany Louise Fenwick (9)	131
Joshua Ufiegbe (8)	132
Sophie Brown (8)	134
Maja Anna Kertesz (8)	135
Nikola Joanna Ojrzynska (9)	136
Lilly Youngson (9)	137
Majka Nicole Dzieza (9)	138
Holly Robertson (8)	139
Kenzie Innes (9)	140
Cally Hannah MacDonald (9)	141
Adam Tomczakowski (9)	142
Charley Laing (9)	143
Maja Swiderska (9)	144
Kayla-Marie O'Driscoll (9)	145

Royal Blind School, Edinburgh

Bo Cox (7)	146
Rebeka Ritchie (11)	148

St Leonards School, The Pends

Archie Donaldson (9)	149
Lana McGuire (9)	150
Emily Rose Anderson (8)	152
Conor MacKay (9)	153
Willow Manifold (10)	154
Verity Swift (9)	155
Cameron Duncan (9)	156
Ben Alexander Smeddle (8)	157
Lewis Hanton (9)	158
Jonny Chernin (8)	159
Aidan Jon MacKay (7)	160
Julius Gill (8)	161
Francis Maughan (8)	162
Theo Gautreau (7)	163
Simon Schwoebel (8)	164

St Roch's RC Primary School, Glasgow

Ayomide Olawuyi (9)	165
Sonia Kester (9)	166

Cara Trainer (9)	167
Javaid Naqvi (8)	168
Ryan Liu (8)	169
Arshad Mughery (9)	170
Victor Akintula (9)	171
Yu Fan Li (9)	172
Shabib Khan (8)	173
Natnael Tekle (9)	174
Callum McDermid (9)	175
Andy Chen (9)	176

Strathpeffer Primary School, Strathpeffer

Logan Iain Anderson (9)	177
Laura MacDonald (10)	178
Eilidh Scott (10)	179
Jessica Emily Cameron (10)	180
Sophie Kay (10)	181
Sarah Amaya Decarole Butler-Whittaker (10)	182
Hew Rasdale (10)	183
Freya Waite (9)	184
James MacGillivray (10)	186
Katie Jankowski (10)	187
Brooke Mackenzie (10)	188
Ruby Frame (10)	189
Keira Syrjanen (10)	190
Finlee Irvine (9)	191
Ellie-Rose Scott (10)	192
Connie Mackain (10)	193

★ The Poems ★

The Flanders Fields

Flanders fields, the poppies everywhere
They sway about, the beautiful red poppies
The poppies are red like the soldier's blood
They remind me of the soldiers
I am proud of all of the soldiers but I am also sad,
They sacrificed their lives for us.

Flanders fields, the bombs are dropping
everywhere
Feeling terrible at the sight of death
Gunshots and screaming is all I hear
Depression of soldiers losing their friends
Blood flowing like a river
In Flanders fields.

I will remember all the soldiers
Who fought and died to save our country
Every day I take a minute to think
How brave they were to the world
All the tears are shed
In Flanders fields.

Ela Kudret Arican (9)
Alexandra Parade Primary School, Dennistoun

Worst World War

World War One, worst world war.

Everyone knew we were loved
But then realised it's every man for himself.

The diseases are dangerous
While everyone is fumbling around for ardent glory.

Unexpectedly, scalding hot shrapnel
Falls from the smoke-corrupted sky.

Death. Screams. Cries.

In all of my dreams, I knew
I was going to serve my country but not this way...

Bang!

Mud throws up into the air
Like a pantomime about miracles.

While our cursed, haunted faces
Grow more evil as they shoot.

The incurable faith of the enemies grow stronger
As the cursed tanks fire away...

Silence starts to awaken
In the muddy compound.

"Hurrah!" shout the men
As they stumble to hug each other.

Bloodshot eyes
Wring to the back of heads.

Innocent, cursed-looking foes limp
Onto the battlefield as they look for ardent glory.

The smoke-corrupted sky
Starts to clear.

Iman Adewunmi (10)
Alexandra Parade Primary School, Dennistoun

Oh, The Lovely Poppies

Oh, the lovely poppies,
In the battlefields, I wish I could go take them
But if I did, I would die
And have to say goodbye.

The first of the war passes,
As slowly as they say,
As time ticks, the more soldiers we lose,
It brings tears to my eyes.

Soldiers limping and rushing
Their way through the trench,
Soldiers getting ready to shoot
Soldiers lying dead on the bloody floor,
Soldiers playing cards.

It's horrible here
It's muddy, dirty, bloody, stinks of oil
Canned food, smoke and more.

I can't sleep
I'm thinking of what
The Germans may do to me

I miss home, I miss Mother and Father
I can hear them coming
I hear them...

They are here
They are here
Oh, the lovely poppies
In the battlefields.

Lexie Fraser (10)
Alexandra Parade Primary School, Dennistoun

How It Feels

Bullets flying by
You know how I feel
People dying every single time
I snap my fingers or breathe in and out.

Grenades dropping into our trenches...
Bang!

Blood spatters over me and my friends
Why did we sign up for this?

Gas every day and no sleep
I wish I was home to relax.

All I see and do is run, shoot,
Talk and play cards sometimes.

I also hear and smell
People screaming, talking and shooting
It smells like mud, gunpowder
Blood and rotten feet.

Trust me, you don't want to be here
It is like hell in no-man's-land.

Georgi Mitev (9)
Alexandra Parade Primary School, Dennistoun

War

World War One, the worst war of all
The devastating destruction on fields
The petrifying sounds of gunshots and bombs
What I have seen, I can't get out of my head
The tanks were really badly made.

We were moving up enemy lines
"I see some German troops!" I shouted
We snuck through our trenches
Then we attacked
We thought we got the upper hand
But we were wrong.

There was a green mist coming towards us
We all shouted, "Gas!"
Some of us got our gas masks on
Some did not - I did, it was terrible
What you have seen will give you PTSD.

Rhys Byrne (10)
Alexandra Parade Primary School, Dennistoun

Terrible Trenches

Terrible trenches, red blood
Around dead bodies lying on the ground
Smells so bad
Trenches are muddy
Not one single buddy.
Here it is, the day has come
Lying on the ground with everyone
And soldiers stomping all around.

Ruby-red river full of blood
Starved, scared soldiers
Hiding in the trenches
Constant gunshots all around
Digging holes in the ground.

At night we fight against the Germans
Take them by surprise
Not expecting it
Not organised
They can't fight back
Here comes a gas attack.

Summer Kennedy Haigh (10)
Alexandra Parade Primary School, Dennistoun

Battle Of The Somme

It is the first day
I am not expecting to go over to fight.
I am trudging in the mud
To get ready to fight
Right now, I am scared.

"Over the top!" says the general
We all go out of the trenches
To no-man's-land.

I hear bombs shooting
Smell of smoke
"It is not affecting the enemies."

The Germans hear us
They are using the German machine guns
My friends are dying
"Help! Help!" yell all my friends.

I am alone,
I can hear myself
I am scared.

Loveena Mathew Thomas (10)
Alexandra Parade Primary School, Dennistoun

War!

W orld has changed, everyone is in shame but
more people are in pain
O pen up, you would see missile craters
everywhere
R ain dropping into the trench
L ying here in all the blood and guts
D eath everywhere.

W ar will end but not today
A t the battlefield, thousands are dying
R ed blood splattering everywhere.

O ne day I am sure we'll be free
N o-man's-land is awful
E nd is so near.

Reiss Thomas Comrie (9)

Alexandra Parade Primary School, Dennistoun

No-Man's-Land

Every day I hear gunshots in no-man's-land
People shouting, "Help!"
People hiding in the trenches
Their friends are dying
I don't want to die from the bombs
My mum and dad are dead
I don't want to go outside
Everyone is frightened.

Dents in the grass from explosions
People's dead bodies covered in blood
I'm scared, terrified because everyone is dying
I'm sad for the people who have died.

Why are we fighting?

Leah Lee Duffin (9)
Alexandra Parade Primary School, Dennistoun

World War One

W ondering if I will survive
O ver the top is a ticket to death
R unning, trying not to die
L ying still, so I don't die
D eath is where we end.

W ishing that I am home
A poppy is in Flanders fields
R unning to the battlefield.

O n the 11th month, on the 11th day is the end of the war
N asty blood everywhere
E xhausted soldiers at war.

Navtej Natt (10)
Alexandra Parade Primary School, Dennistoun

Trench Troubles

In the trench,
Pools of blood,
Lay like a red carpet,
And in winter,
It turns to red ice
That makes gunshots bounce
To the sky.

Why was I the one to go?
The powerful machine guns are
So loud, it is known
When to run from the smoke
Oh, why me?

Out on no-man's-land
It is squelching with mud and dead bodies
At night, I sit on a sandbag
Thinking about when
I am going to die.

Nadine Mcleod (9)
Alexandra Parade Primary School, Dennistoun

World War One

Why did I come here?
To fight
To be in the army
I thought it would be over
But I was wrong.

I cannot sleep
I cannot eat
I cannot even think straight
No more.

I feel the blood dripping
Dripping all over me
With all the sweat
Running down
My frightened face.

Why did I come here?
To fight
To be in the army
I thought it would be over
But I was wrong.

Molly Hutton (10)
Alexandra Parade Primary School, Dennistoun

The Time Has Come

The war has started,
All the soldiers are risking their lives
There's gunshots everywhere I move.

There's bombs exploding
Guts and fingers flying
All my friends are dying.

But one soldier is choking
Drowning by the poisonous gas.

There's 25 troops left
And there are 40 troops left in the Germans.

It's a hard life down in the trenches
Everybody is scared.

Marcus Kerr (10)
Alexandra Parade Primary School, Dennistoun

The Devil's Sin

The bullets above my head
I know are too close for comfort
All I know
These are the bullets
Of the Devil's sin.

The bombs of the German planes
I fear will drop on me
I fear the bullets
I fear the tanks
Most of all,
I fear the Devil's sin!

When I joined the army
I thought it would be fun
I thought it would be easy
I never did think
Of the Devil's sin.

Dylan Hutchison (9)
Alexandra Parade Primary School, Dennistoun

The Devil's Nightmare

Bang! The German's artillery
Fires at us every day
While our injured
Lay low on no-man's-land
They are left astray
It is too dangerous
To go at this time of day.

Every day, I regret
The day I came here
Every day, I am filled with fear
Why did I ever come here?

These magnetic flowers
Help me stop
Shuddering from fear
Oh, why did
I ever come here?

Riyaan Qadir (10)
Alexandra Parade Primary School, Dennistoun

World War One

W orld War One isn't over yet
O nly some of my friends are living
R ode out to fight
L arge bombs drop
D eath is everywhere.

W as it worth it to come here?
A ll the soldiers want to be home
R ocks are easy to trip on hiding in the mud.

O ne day I will be free from war
N o-man's-land is terrible
E veryone is dead.

Kyle Galasso (10)
Alexandra Parade Primary School, Dennistoun

WWI

One day I woke up in the muddy trench
I woke up because my friend woke me up
My bed was made out of mud and wood
It was so uncomfortable.

Bomb! Bomb! Hide! Phew, that was close
I could no longer cope
This was so not my style
I did not know what was going to happen to me.

I was still trying to run away
Me and my few mates said to man up
I agreed... secretly, I did not.

Ross William Manson (10)
Alexandra Parade Primary School, Dennistoun

World War One

Why have I joined?
I regret every move I have done
Gunfire moving swiftly above my head
No one should deserve the pain
One hesitation can cost my life
The Germans are charging at us.

France are almost retreating.

There is a clear winner... not us
After one hour of gunfire... there is silence
I think it's only me now
I think it's the end, the Germans are here.

Albert Kalmar (10)
Alexandra Parade Primary School, Dennistoun

Blood Shoots

I hear blood shoots every day
People shouting, "Help! Help!"
I fear to sleep, I hope for this war to be over
People dying
Blood gets all over me
I would puke in the trench
I would go home but I can't.

Man on fire haunting me
Did I sign up to this?
Oh no, gas attack, quickly boys
There are bombs, *boom, boom!*
I'm going to have nightmares.

Murtaza Saleem (9)
Alexandra Parade Primary School, Dennistoun

World War One

W ondering if I will survive
O r make it to my trench
R ifles are shooting
L earning new skills along the way
D eath is near.

W hen will it end?
A lways scared and tired
R unning away from the Germans.

O ut in Flanders fields, it's called
N o-man's-land
E xhausted from a long battle.

LJ Nohar (9)

Alexandra Parade Primary School, Dennistoun

WWI

W orld War One has started
O h no, the soldiers are dying
R un for your life!
L ook at the dead soldiers
D ead soldiers, dead.

W hat is happening?
A rghhhh! I almost died
R un, so you do not perish.

O h no, I want to go home
N o! My friend has been shot
E nd the war so I can go home.

Sara Croitoru (10)

Alexandra Parade Primary School, Dennistoun

War Is No Fun

W hy did I join this thing anyway?
O nly idiots would join if they knew
R unning with the general
L ots of dead bodies are lying in the trenches
D on't know if I'm going to die.

W ant to run but I can't
A nd I wish this would end
R emember me if I die.

1 00,000 of us have died already I think.

Tyler Owens (10)
Alexandra Parade Primary School, Dennistoun

World War One The Past Time

How did I get here?
Who made this happen?
I don't like it
Get me out of here!

"Oh no..." someone starts shouting
Bang! Bam!

There are bloodstains
I would love to help but...
Blood is the thing
I don't like.

How did I get up here?
Who made this happen?
I don't like it
Get me out of here!

Ewa Kalinska (10)
Alexandra Parade Primary School, Dennistoun

The Blazing Fields

Why did I sign up for the war?
If I knew just how bad this would be
I would not have signed up!

On the field, we stand for our country
Hoping we will not be killed.

When night falls, I never sleep
Not even a peep.

At dawn, we go over the top
Hoping we will not pop.

Now I'm longing to be at home
Where I like to be.

Nina Peter (10)
Alexandra Parade Primary School, Dennistoun

The Germans Rushed

They are here,
The Germans fierce
And scared, I slowly took
My rifle and stealthily
Walked along
The squelching trenches
As I looked over, I saw...

Before my next word
The Germans were running
Over no-man's-land
Screaming and shouting
Like mad men
As I saw each red poppy
Get squished by
Their big German boots.

Cole O'Neill (10)
Alexandra Parade Primary School, Dennistoun

WWI

W e are in the trenches
O ur soldiers are waiting
R eady to die
L ots of dead men
D ying men screaming.

W ar is scary
A ngry soldiers fighting
R ats biting your skin.

O ne soldier vomiting blood
N o-man's-land is well... no-man's-land
E veryone is dying.

Daniel McWilliamson (9)
Alexandra Parade Primary School, Dennistoun

The War

W hat did I do?
O ur place is muddy
R egret being here
L oud shouting and loud gunshots
D eadly shooting.

W e are tripping over dead bodies
A dead body
R apid gunfire.

O ne of my friends died
N o-man's-land
E veryone is dying as I am speaking.

Melisa Ioana Giuraniuc (10)

Alexandra Parade Primary School, Dennistoun

Death In The War

The war had started
Gunshots and gunshots all the time
Cannons, grenades and bombs every day.

Gas attacks and explosions
Right into the trenches
I'm terrified and scared
There's not many soldiers left
Dead bodies everywhere
Just as well as blood.

Every time we try to cross
We just get machine-gunned down.

Jayden Spencer (10)
Alexandra Parade Primary School, Dennistoun

World War One

W hat am I doing here?
O ur place is full of dirt and water
R apid gun firing
L ord, I hate the war
D ead bodies everywhere.

W ar is so bad
A re dead bodies everywhere?
R ats in the trenches.

O pen field
N oble soldiers
E xcitement over victory.

Trevor James McCarry (10)
Alexandra Parade Primary School, Dennistoun

War

W e are in the trenches
O ur soldiers are waiting
R eady to die
L ots of dead men
D ying man screaming.

W ar is scary
A ngry soldiers fighting
R ats biting our skin.

O ne soldier vomiting blood
N o-man's-land is awful
E veryone is dying.

Bethany Jane Reid (10)
Alexandra Parade Primary School, Dennistoun

The War

W ar has struck
O n our way to die
R unning for our lives
L ike dying birds
D id the war stop yet?

W hy world,
A re men dying?
R ed blood everywhere.

O ne day, I wish to return home
N ever make me do this again
E nd this war now!

Sarah Benedetti (10)
Alexandra Parade Primary School, Dennistoun

World War One

W ild smoke
O ver the top shouting
R elief that I survived
L oud screaming
D aring and brave.

W onder what happens next
A wful, tragic and intense
R unning for their lives.

O ver in the trenches
N ot happy
E motion!

Safaa Ahmed (9)
Alexandra Parade Primary School, Dennistoun

The Great War

How did I get here?
When did I get here?
Why am I here?

The gigantic German tanks
And the soldiers are here,
As I run, they just keep
On firing the horrid
Bullets at me.

I don't like the bang
Noises from them.

They just keep on
Shooting
Powerful
Bullets.

Vincent Wang (9)
Alexandra Parade Primary School, Dennistoun

The Great War!

The Germans are here
All I can hear is
Bombs, gunshots and much more!
Why am I here?
Why am I doing this?

I can't sleep
The noise is awful
I'm scared
As time is ticking
People are dying.

The Germans are here
For revenge
It brings me to tears
Oh dear!

Reese Jaffray (9)
Alexandra Parade Primary School, Dennistoun

The War To End All Wars

Why am I here?
This place is horrible
I could die any minute
The Germans are back.

They're coming
Over the top
I might die now
We are going to battle.

I killed a German
The British are dying fast
But so are they.

If they surrender,
We have won.

Lewis Watson (10)
Alexandra Parade Primary School, Dennistoun

The Tragic War

Why did I want to come here?
What have I done?
Everyone shaking in the trench
Because of the bodies all around.

Suddenly, I see an unfriendly horse
Escape from where it is found.

Then I look up at the battlefield
And my friends could not be found.

Courtney Anderson (10)
Alexandra Parade Primary School, Dennistoun

Regrets

What have I done?
Why am I in a war?
Why did I do this?

Enemies come, friends go
Having blood dripping everywhere
Guns firing, people dying,
But still, somehow poppies grow.

Everyone yelling and stumbling
So sick of life
Why me? Why me?

Jessica Margaret Strachan (10)
Alexandra Parade Primary School, Dennistoun

The Poppy

P oppies were made for Remembrance Day

O ur mums and dads and grandparents wear poppies too

P eople wear poppies all around the world

P oppies are very special for soldiers

Y ou can buy a poppy for Remembrance.

Safoora Sarwar (10)

Alexandra Parade Primary School, Dennistoun

World War One

It's very cold in the trench
I wonder why I am here
There are so many dead bodies.

We all dream
The war will finish
But it never does...

When we see poppies
We feel better.

Charlie Blair (10)
Alexandra Parade Primary School, Dennistoun

Gold

Golden watches glittering on the shelves
Golden charms jingling on a bracelet
Golden cheese from the farm
Golden lights glittering at Christmas
Golden tables for the party
Golden leaves falling from the trees in autumn
Golden crown on the king
Golden stars glittering
Golden medals for the winners
Gold, happy, rich, shiny and bright.

Ryan McDonald (8)
Aultmore Park Primary School, Glasgow

Pink

I love raspberry ice lollies and pink candyfloss
They are both so yummy
Sweet strawberries and raspberries
Are healthy fruit to eat when I am hungry
I have shy, pink cheeks when I meet new friends
Pink flowers and tulips, roses too
I just love them all.
Pink blusher on my cheeks
Barbies and unicorns, magical hair and the pink
world.

Brooke Clark (8)

Aultmore Park Primary School, Glasgow

Red

Delicious, red strawberries in my tummy
Red danger card stop!
Red spicy peppers, hot, hot, hot!
Red blazing hot fire in winter
Red, luscious lipstick, very glamorous and very shiny
Lovely red roses
Summer, the time to have strawberry ice lollies, yum!

Lucy Donnelly (8)
Aultmore Park Primary School, Glasgow

Yellow

Sun shining brightly
In the morning when the sun comes up
Fluffy yellow chicks
Just born in spring
Leaves yellow in autumn
Big bunches of bananas
Yellow traffic light - like a big Smartie
Yellow lollipops, lovely lemon, yum!

Olivia Craig (7)
Aultmore Park Primary School, Glasgow

Yellow

Yummy cheese for lunch
The sun shining brightly
Bananas yummy
Nice, smiling sunflowers
Busy bees in their hives
People eating yolky egg
Lemons and pineapples, sunshine fruits
Yellow is a cosy colour.

Shayne-Patrick Devine (7)
Aultmore Park Primary School, Glasgow

Yellow

The sun is a star
Yellow beams warming us
Warm, soothing
Wrapping us in heat
Sunflower opens up
Beautiful
Bowls of pasta from Italy
Mamma mia!
Yellow, soft, gooey like custard.

Joseph Andrew Murdoch (7)
Aultmore Park Primary School, Glasgow

Blue

Lovely blue sky,
Cold sea,
Big blueberries growing
Write with blue Biro pens
Artists start to paint with blue paint
Blue box full of toys
Blue tray full of blue paper.

Yu Chen Weng (7)
Aultmore Park Primary School, Glasgow

Yellow

Cheese and pineapple for my lunch
Bananas hanging on the trees
Going to the beach on a sunny day
I saw a beehive with some busy bees
Happy sunflowers.

George Blair (8)
Aultmore Park Primary School, Glasgow

Black

Black night sky
Darkness everywhere
Witches' pointy hats
Scary black
Black Coke, fizzy and cold in my mouth
Black is sadness.

Oluwagbotemi Kuti (6)
Aultmore Park Primary School, Glasgow

Scary School

S omething felt strange as I strolled into school

C ould there be something happening in my class?

A voice said, "Run away!" then faded like dust,

R egularly, this doesn't happen, am I sleeping?

Y ou know on a normal school day that this doesn't happen.

S chool is empty, where is everybody?

C an you wake me up if I am sleeping?

"H elp!" my voice echoed around the room

O nly if I was sleeping I would stay here,

O nly if there was someone here with me

L ater that evening, I went home.

What will happen on Monday?

Imogen Thomson (8)
Beattock Primary School, Beattock

The Train Of Dreams

T he magnificent moon awaits
R apidly, the train thunders down the track
A n amazing new journey to see
I n the morning, the train is in the desert
N ow the journey is in the clouds
S oaring through the spectacular sky.

J oy is all over the passengers' faces
O bese chocolate bars
U nder silver wrappers they eat
R eady to devour all the treats
N ow hyper children run
E veryone had the best of fun
Y our journey on the train of dreams.

Chloe Harris (8)
Beattock Primary School, Beattock

The One Stop Shop

This vending machine looks suspicious!
Holy moly, what is that?
Anyone seeing this?

Oh, it's a teleporter!
No, no, no! I'm not going in there!
Anyone want to volunteer?

So no one, fine I'll do it
Through I go
Oh, so as soon as I say I'll go, it's even more scary
Phew! It's over!

Some place I'm in
Hip Hop World! Bye-bye
Okay, it's done
Pay for chocolate... and done.

Cameron Fergusson Christie (9)
Beattock Primary School, Beattock

Birthday Boy

B rilliant, the day is here
I never thought it would come
R ight, I need to get dressed
T his is going to be fun
H ave I got presents, Mum?
D own the stairs, I go
A t the bottom, I see my...
Y es, there's trillions of presents around me.

B irthday cake was delicious
O ooh, what is that?
Y es it is, it's one more present!

Kiera Minto (11)
Beattock Primary School, Beattock

Super Rabbit

S uper Rabbit loves flying in the air
U nder the clouds, up so high
P rotects people from the bad
E rupts the bad guys with love
R abbit saves the world.

R abbit runs for the bad guys
A nd rescues every other rabbit in the world
B est rabbit in the world
B est super rabbit ever
I t can save our world
T hanks, Super Rabbit.

Alfie Thomson (9)
Beattock Primary School, Beattock

Do The Elvis Presley

Everyone wearing leather with slick black hair,
Wobbling and dancing like they don't care,
"Hunka, hunka," everyone said,
Disco lights with the colour red,
An Elvis sandwich of banana and peanut butter,
"What a strange favourite," people do mutter,
Seven billion people dancing along,
Arguing about their favourite song
Elvis Presley is the best
Better than all the rest.

Erin Shannon (9)
Beattock Primary School, Beattock

The Flash King

I can hear the people sing
To the king with all the bling
And he is weighed down with gold
And he doesn't do exercise because he is too old.

I can see the flash king
With all the bling
Think of the people who are hungry and cold
Why can't the king share his gold?

Brandon Hughes (11)
Beattock Primary School, Beattock

Chocolate World

Chocolate World is the place to be
I hear bubbles coming down the streams
I smell delicious butterscotch and caramel
I can pick chocolate trees
I can taste chocolate clouds in the sky
I can see chocolate houses
Would you like to come to Chocolate World?

Bethany Anderson (10)
Beattock Primary School, Beattock

Superman

(Haiku poetry)

Now I can fly and
Now I have laser vision,
Super cold breath too.

I am Superman
I am in the Justice League
And with Batman too.

I am from Krypton
In a suit of red and blue
It's time to fight crime!

Alfie Hughes (9)
Beattock Primary School, Beattock

Wizard World

Wizard World is very, very creepy and dangerous
They ride on broomsticks and have amazing wands
They make spectacular spells with their magic
wands
Watch out for the dragon that breathes toxic fire
Do you dare to enter Wizard World?

Tegan Rose Mcclelland (8)
Beattock Primary School, Beattock

The Burger The Size Of Saturn

The burger is huge, the burger is gigantic
I can't believe it is in space
It's bigger than Saturn, that's just crazy
It's bigger than any planet
It's bigger than the Marlner Centre
It's covered in green ketchup, it tastes liquidy
There are orange tomatoes, that's just weird
There are big buns, there are gherkins
There are weird dots on the bun
They are sesame seeds and I don't like them
They are disgusting!
There is salad inside, the salad is red
That is really weird
Every hour, the cheeseburger turns around in space.

Zach Finlayson (8)
Carmuirs Primary School, Camelon

Unicorns And Mermaids

The unicorn sparkles and shines,
It glitters through the night
When the stars are dull and down
The unicorn dazzles so bright.

The unicorn is cool and glows,
Its colour changes peach, purple and red,
And people can see it so clear,
And notice the horn on its head.

The unicorn goes to her castle,
To see her special friend,
She is a fish-tailed mermaid,
With a lot of money to spend.

They go to the shops,
And buy crystal jewels,
Rubies, diamonds, sapphires and more
And give them to children in the local school.

Tiegan McLaughlan (9)
Carmuirs Primary School, Camelon

Crazy Teacher

The crazy teacher always wears pom-poms,
A pom-pom top,
A pom-pom shirt,
Pom-pom shoes,
Pom-pom earrings,
Pom-pom skirt.

Wherever she goes, her pom-poms wriggle,
And she jingles like Santa's sleigh.

The crazy teacher's hair is frizzy
She is a wacky teacher every day.

But one day, some pom-poms fell off,
And the teacher started to cry
But the boys and girls they searched
And saw them floating in the sky.

Aleisha Brown (10)
Carmuirs Primary School, Camelon

Strange World

S hiny and delicious, I sit by the tree
T elekinesis is the life for me
R ainbows forever, beautiful and thinner
A lovely world I wouldn't change anything forever
N ever forever
G reedy whenever
E ating candy.

W ow, we were all fine and dandy
O pening but not closing
R elaxing and dozing
L oving and snowing
D reaming and snoring, amazing!

Claudia Scobbie (9)
Carmuirs Primary School, Camelon

The Liquorice Shark

L ike a non-original shark,
I found a different one,
Q ueen of them all,
U nder the sea lives Oliver,
O h, you better be scared!
R ight where the coral lies,
I n the dark night
C an you watch out?
E at your happy thoughts.

B e ready
I t's scary
T ell me no!
E eeek! They'e coming for me!

Roxanne Jones (9)
Carmuirs Primary School, Camelon

The Rock And The Pink Water

I was sitting on the beach,
And was feeling like a drink,
I saw a bumpy rock,
Full of water that was pink!

I started to drink it,
It tasted so yummy,
I gulped a few mouthfuls,
Then started to act funny.

I told lots of jokes,
And laughed 'til I fell,
I bumped my head,
On that rock and did yell!

Cody Clark (9)
Carmuirs Primary School, Camelon

Chocolate Aeroplane

You go in the plane like a flame,
It's no ordinary plane, it's a chocolate plane,
The big blast is so fast,
When the plane goes so fast, you'll want to blast
When it flies so smooth, you don't want to move
Do you want to go in my chocolate plane?

Arran Frederick (8)
Carmuirs Primary School, Camelon

Candy Classrooms

C andy classrooms are the best
A mazing candy classrooms from Candy Land
N erdz, Haribo, Skittles, Rolos, Hershey's Kisses
D on't each too much or it will make you sick
Y um yum! Delicious!

Ryan Walsh (9)
Carmuirs Primary School, Camelon

Bouncy Cookie

The big, bouncy cookie sits in a big tub of milk,
Small chocolate chips white as teeth
I take a bite, I keep on eating
Oh no, now I'm floating up to the sun!
Magic chocolate chips, they've made me lighter
than air!

Owen Sommerville (9)
Carmuirs Primary School, Camelon

My Weird Adventure

I ran a race on Saturn
In a zigzag pattern
Me and my friends did a relay with rings
It felt like I had silky wings.
I danced about but slipped and fell
Then I transported into a well
I ached all over with my mouth shut
And then I banged my poor, poor butt!
On Pluto, I heard mooing cows
They had noisy rows
On Mercury, the grunting pigs
Had blue, curly wigs
On Venus, the barking dogs
Were sitting on talking logs,
On Uranus, the cute ducks
Were on bright yellow trucks
I shrugged inside the well
Ouch, I feel as hard as a shell
Finally, back down to Earth
I sobbed, missed out the mirth.

Erin Harnett (8)
Cults Primary School, Cults

A Dancing Elephant On The Moon

A huge elephant was on the moon,
When suddenly, we all heard a *boom!*

We looked at the moon, it had cracked,
But the silly elephant kept on dancing until he got trapped.

Cracked and trapped! Oh deary me
We were all scared but all the elephants wanted was a cup of tea.

The tea went *splash*,
And the cups went *crash!*

The tea started to dance
The elephant and the moon jumped around and pranced.

What a crazy dancing elephant he was!

Artemy Melgui (9)
Cults Primary School, Cults

The Weird Things I Saw In A Hot Air Balloon

In a hot air balloon I saw:
A lady walking her giraffe on the sun
A ceilidh on Pluto that looked like fun
A monster on Mars that was eating bars
And then he was fascinated by lots of stars.
The lady and her giraffe were finished their walk
When suddenly, the giraffe started to talk!
"Oh my, oh my, I am tired and now
Let's go home, let's go right now!"
I followed them down and got home at last
And now it's all in the past.

Ava Skinner (9)
Cults Primary School, Cults

The Talking Instruments

On stage in the Sydney Opera House,
Was a band, The Talking Instruments
The guitar stood up and said, "Hello Australia!"
Then the drums stood up and shouted, "Let's go!"
The crowd cheered
The saxophone stood up and said,
"We're going to sing our bestseller."
It was the best night ever
In the Sydney Opera House.

James Street (9)
Cults Primary School, Cults

A Shark

I was at the park when I saw a shark
It was not even dark
I whispered, "That's weird,
Does it have a beard?"
It flew up in the sky
Up, up, so high in the sky,
The shark's teeth glowed
The wind really blew,
"I'll call you Blossom."
The shark said, "That's awesome."

Wajeeha Hamid (9)
Cults Primary School, Cults

Elloanus

Have you heard the girl called Elloanus,
Who coughed out a unicorn in Uranus?
Did you know he ate unicorn soup
Whilst spinning with a hula hoop?
She span and span and span,
Whilst frying an egg in a pan.
She invited an elf to tea
But he only wanted a pea,
She invited a fairy,
Who was called Mysterious Mary!

Fatema Gomaa (9)
Cults Primary School, Cults

Stairs To The Moon

I was climbing the stairs to the moon
To be the first one with a spoon
To taste the nice moon cheese
But I heard a big *boom!*
The stairs were collapsing
I needed to get away soon
I could see the stairs behind me going faster than a lion
So I jumped off the stairs
Then landed in my room.

Ben Smart (9)
Cults Primary School, Cults

The Futuristic Visit

A spaceship crashed in my backyard,
I went to check it out
It was a car from the year 3000.

The door opened, it was a... a... a...
Human from the future!
He needed my help as he was injured
I gave him medicine
He felt good
We flew off in his car to his planet.

Yaseen Zweit (9)
Cults Primary School, Cults

The Olive

I woke up in an olive and began to eat it
I peered through and saw
A beautiful butterfly
I jumped on and he flew me
To a pool of glimmering water
I got out of the water and
Jumped in a couple more times
I dried off in the sun
And the butterfly flew me home.

Keanna Couch (9)
Cults Primary School, Cults

Sports Day On The Moon

It was sports day on the moon
All the aliens were there
They were green and gloopy
They did a relay race.

They were running, jogging and hopping
Aliens were waving their flags
There were thousands of aliens cheering
It was a great day for sports day.

Hollie Chalmers (8)
Cults Primary School, Cults

Riding On A Unicorn

One day when I came home,
A unicorn was in my room!
I jumped on its back and off we flew
We passed the magical moon
The unicorn was sparkly and shimmery
She did the floss with me
We had cotton candy and strawberry ice cream
And then I went home for tea.

Lucy MacDonald (9)
Cults Primary School, Cults

Draco's Travels

I'm in the sky, oh no!
I got hit by a pie
I landed in Dubai
Me and Draco said, "Goodbye."
We travelled all the way to Africa
Me and Draco did the conga
Then we went camping for two
We zoomed home and said, "Toodaloo."

Taha Zweit (9)
Cults Primary School, Cults

Today I Flew Home On A Sofa

Today I flew home on a sofa
People stared in shock
I felt cool as I zoomed past
Waving my hands as I went
The wind swished on my face
As I raced birds through the sky
I landed on my driveway
And said, "Cheerio sofa!"

Gavin Pedrog (9)
Cults Primary School, Cults

My Rainbow

Today I ate a rainbow
I got it from McRainbows
I was about to take a bite
When a little mite
Came and took a bite
And said
"Have a little laugh
And eat this rainbow with me."

Sienna Herd (8)
Cults Primary School, Cults

My Crazy Monkey On The Moon

My crazy monkey on the moon
Riding a spoon
While humming a tune
She'll be leaving soon
From the super moon
On the 30th of June.

Nika Sharifi (8)
Cults Primary School, Cults

Ninja Ice Cream

Once there was a time before the Big Bang
No one could talk, they just said, "Ying Yong Yang."
There was no school, the only actual liquid was in a
pool
There were suns for hire and not a single light
But one time, this land was attacked
They even made it past the barracks
They made it clear they were the bosses here
So for once in forever, they had to release the
Ninja Dude Guy,
Who taught them a lesson for messin' around
He sent them away but no one said 'yay'
The place was wrecked so they started to rebuild
But it wasn't very good since nobody could go to
school
So they did their best to build one
And while all this going on
Ninja Dude Guy was making an edible version of
himself
That you would know as ice cream.

Adam Balanowski (9)
Echline Primary School, South Queensferry

The Sea Party

One day in the special sea
There was a party
Splash and splosh, they were having a party
It was a sea party
They wanted their party to last all night
With no fights
They loved parties, especially their own
With no traffic cones
They even invited the sea yeti
Called Beti
It was finally time to dance
It was a great chance
It was party time
Time to rhyme
Everyone came, even Beti
The yeti
It was so fun
They were eating plums.

Olivia Ferguson (9)
Echline Primary School, South Queensferry

Weird World

Once, a long time ago, in a land
Where there was no sand,
There were unicorns for people,
Their pavement was purple.
Would you like this?
You will go *whizz!*
They had candy buildings, weird!
They heard everything.
They had cloud animals that could talk,
They could walk,
They had wings.
They had to go to bed when the bell dings.

Ding!

Isobel Buckley (9)
Echline Primary School, South Queensferry

A Little Magic

I live in a land of no limit
It is fun under the sun
Dragons are around and soar
They let out a mighty roar.

Wetlands all around
Big craters in volcano surrounds
Burning lava lake
That looks like an orange cake.

I have hands that choose powers
As gentle as flowers
They can be magic and fast
They go off with a blast.

In my magical land.

Shay Alexander Hand (9)
Echline Primary School, South Queensferry

The Swimming Pool

One day, a guy with a rainbow spider costume
went swimming
He was gleaming with joy
When he went to take his boy
And his costume was a green elephant
When they jumped in the pool
They met a walking ghoul
When he got his ring
The ghoul took her things and left
And gobbled his food
Then bobbled his head.

Jack Crow (9)
Echline Primary School, South Queensferry

Football

Hi, I am a walking, talking football
I am very small,
You can kick me high and you can watch me fall.
I can go high because if you kick me
I can fly in the sky.
I see birds in the sky
That is because I am up so high
On my way back down to the ground
All I make is a crashing sound.

Caleb Munro (9)
Echline Primary School, South Queensferry

Rainbow Yeti

Once there was a rainbow yeti
And his name was Beti
He loved spaghetti
He said, "I get spaghetti."
He liked chasing rainbows
He had lots of bows
He lived in a lagoon
And he loved a rainbow balloon
He loved the flying cheese
Because he loved to say cheese.

Katie Hughes (9)
Echline Primary School, South Queensferry

Underwater Jungle

Jungles have Beagles
That fly around like eagles
The monkeys are whining
Because they want to go dining
The jaguar is sneaking
Because it wants to be eating
The waves are fast
But don't be last
The jungle is big
But it has lots of figs.

Connell Walker (9)
Echline Primary School, South Queensferry

The School In A Potato

As I walked in the charming field
A potato was running around like a wheel
I stepped on the potato and I went *poof!*
I went *bang* as the ground went *woof!*

I went to the classroom, I was looking blue
It was moist and soggy as I discovered it was a
school
The teacher was tired of smelling the old potato.

Finally, it was lunch
I tried the potato broth, it was putrid but it was my
brunch
So I ate some potato crisps
It was plain and dull but luckily, had some bits.

The lunch hall rumbled as someone was pelting it
Through the window, I saw a mitt
We jumped out the potato and we were out
What a day!

Rebecca Murtagh (11)
Falla Hill Primary School, Fauldhouse

Tropical Sweet Planet

On the tropical sweet planet,
I was blinded by the bonbon sun.

Everything on this planet cooked so much fun
The Dorito palm trees were tall
The chocolate beach was soft
How badly I wanted to eat it all!

The sweet gumdrop rain
Revealing an astonishing Haribo rainbow.

On the tropical sweet planet,
I heard the gumdrop rain splashing the chocolate
river
The noise was so nice, it could stop pain.

On the tropical sweet planet,
I could smell all the delicious sweets
From the milk chocolate river
Coming to this planet
You won't need to bring treats.

On the tropical sweet planet,
I waddled over to the chocolate river

And had a drink
It tasted like a dream, it was so good
It would make you scream.

Sean McDonald (11)
Falla Hill Primary School, Fauldhouse

House Of Cards

Have you ever been in a house
A huge house of cards
And running the house is a very large mouse?
People play with your walls
Shuffle them and fall
I open up the door
But cards fall to the floor
People pick them up
And say, "That's good luck."
When people walk past
I need to be fast
It smells like raw fish
When people wash the dish
At dinner last night
There was a big, big fight
Someone won and someone lost
Someone will pay a big cost
I took a nibble of a card
But it was really, really hard
Banging and shouting all around
All people can do is drop a pound

They pick the pound up and go to the shop
And when they come home, they're carrying a
mop.

Sarah McLean Abbott (11)

Falla Hill Primary School, Fauldhouse

Pokémon Costa

I went to my local shop
Hoping for nice, warm drinks
Coming and going
Went the swarm of people.

It was the Pokémon Costa
Fire, water, grass and fifteen other types
It's a wonderful taste, particularly Drowzee
All so delicious.

The cup was smooth
Hard to know it was in my hands
Magical, dark and super tough
One was really hard.

I could hear the bubbling drink
Melting some ice type
Bashing, throwing each other down into my cup
It was a blender filling up in one drop.

Smells delicious as I put it down my throat
My mouth burning from the fire inside

Smelt like the coal, I'll put the burning smoke out
The smoke came out of my nostrils.

Charlie Bruce Allen (10)

Falla Hill Primary School, Fauldhouse

Underwater Dragon Zoo

The cages were big
And the dragons were tall
But I did not want to
Step into this zoo at all!

The dragon's teeth were sharp
And its skin was dark
The fire shot out
As fast as a shark.

His breathing was loud
And the bubbles were round
Why am I in here?
I thought as I frowned.

Its eyes were bright
And its nose was light
But the dragon looked
Like it wanted a fight!

I think I will go
And leave this place

But I should say goodbye
To the dragon's face!

So wish me luck
As I leave today
Goodbye everyone
While I watch the dragon lay.

Alexander Cook (10)

Falla Hill Primary School, Fauldhouse

Unicorn Land

U nicorns are amazing
N o flamingoes allowed
I see slime and squishies
C orn is their favourite food
O r they like candy
R ainbows are cool
N o mermaids allowed.

S lime is fluffy
L ove unicorns
I see unicorns
M e and unicorns are kind together
E verybody loves unicorns.

I see love and kindness
S ome people have unicorns.

R ainbows have unicorns in them

A pple

I can party

N o bullying unicorns

B ows are worn

O n Saturday, I swim with unicorns

W ow!

Amber Gourlay (10)

Falla Hill Primary School, Fauldhouse

Running On Water

R un, run, run away, run as fast as I can

U p the wave and down again, *splash splash!*

N ever going to stop

N o, no, no, no, they are still there

I 've got to run, run, run even faster

N ee-naw, nee-naw, where did he go? Down the sewer

G reat they found me, now I have to run up the sewers, ewww yuck!

O h, oh, here comes a smelly octopus

N o, no, no, not me, them!

W hat, just call a boat so we can catch him

A nd that's all I need

T hey're blocking all the exits

E hhh, ah-ha!

R un, run, run, finally escaped.

Leah Brand (10)
Falla Hill Primary School, Fauldhouse

Rainbow Ride To The Moon

I waited patiently at the bus stop
For the bus to arrive until...
Rumble, rumble, the ground was shaking
I dropped to the ground and a tiny sprout of colours
Popped out from the ground
It was a rainbow
"Hop on," it said, I got up and so I did.

I shot up into the bright blue sky
The bright, lemon sun shone in the fluffy clouds.

The sky started to become darker and darker
"I think I'm heading for the moon."

I soared past the pointy glowing starts until
I hit a jawbreaker like boulder
I fell with a slam and a bump
What do I know, I'm on the moon.

Dylan Rae (10)
Falla Hill Primary School, Fauldhouse

Saucy Steamy Spicy Steak

Bigger than the Titanic, the steak she made
Tender, stringy and strong the steak was,
Chewed up, my mouth it stayed,
Sizzle! Pop! Fizz! Everyone dived into the delicious steak.

Firm, silky, soft, I fainted onto it
Magnificent, I sank into the juicy steak, not thinking
It was as airy, soft and delicious as a ball pit
Drooling and gazing at a hole
I really thought it could fit.

Like a million BBQs it smelt,
So supreme it must be fake
In my mouth, it did melt
Rapidly I swallowed,
But just amazing, the aftertaste felt.

Adrian Macrae (11)
Falla Hill Primary School, Fauldhouse

Buger House

B urger House, your favourite place ever
U se your hands and feet with caution
R un but not too fast
G et a plate 'cause your dinner's here
E at the door, windows or even the walls
R egular houses are boring, this one is interesting.

H ouses are inedible but this is edible
O ut the house, in the door, you won't get bored
U se a fork and knife but don't eat the house
S ee the different types of burgers
E ating it like a McDonald's and the neighbours
join in.

Thomas Charles William Swan (11)
Falla Hill Primary School, Fauldhouse

Gooey Gremlin Earwax

I cleaned a gremlin's ears, "Oh yuck!"
Sticky and oozy, mouldy and green
I was really out of luck
I took another big blob out
Then I heard a mutter
"Fista, wista, mista, muff."
Next, I heard a splutter
I saw a cube of bright, white stuff
Then the gremlin ate it
"A marshmallow!" I exclaimed
The gremblin grumbled, "So?"
"Say that spell when I say to...
"Go!"
Me and the gremlin had a feast
Roasted, toasted marshmallows!
I was the luckiest person in the east!

Grace Blair (10)
Falla Hill Primary School, Fauldhouse

Lollipop Land

L and of pops, eating a lollipop
O n the moon and it sucked me up
L aughing and giggling down a slide
L aughing too hard, could not stop
I n Lollipop Land, it is fun
P opping and sizzling, crunching in Lollipop Land
O fficially in Lollipop Land, fun and games
P op! What was that? A balloon popped.

L ollipop Land, I love the crunch and sizzle
A lollipop was bigger than my head
N ow it is time to go
D own the slide, back to the moon.

Sophie Robertson (11)
Falla Hill Primary School, Fauldhouse

Cotton Candy Tree

I live in a cotton candy tree
What do I see?
I see a giant cotton candy bed.

I live in a cotton candy tree
I hear children chomping cheerfully
At my house
While I was lying in my soft, fluffy bed.

I live in a cotton candy tree
What do I feel?
I feel something
That felt rather like a cloud.

I live in a cotton candy tree
I smell sweet, sugary, soft fluff.

I live in a cotton candy tree
I taste sweet, delicious sugar.

Elle Wightman (10)
Falla Hill Primary School, Fauldhouse

Scotland On The Moon

Scotland felt weird,
I didn't feel safe,
It felt bad,
I was dizzy,
Night lasted long,
The sun was visible but didn't show light
The Earth was in sight,
I soon found out that I was on the moon,
I could breathe without oxygen,
It was cold,
School was floaty,
We all floated,
I floated in my sleep,
Life is so hard on the moon,
Then I fell,
Then I floated into space,
Life was so hard on the moon.

Abigail Mclernon (10)
Falla Hill Primary School, Fauldhouse

It's Raining Cookies

Cookies are falling from the sky
I see them with my little eye
Some are all crunchy and munchy
"Oww, I got hurt."
With a little squirt
It stopped raining cookies and started pouring with rain
"Oh," the people said
They started running
Looking for shelter
"Ewww, that smell of rain is disgusting."
"Arghhhh, the rain is cold."
"Arghhhh, it's windy and blowing me about."

Maci Carty (10)
Falla Hill Primary School, Fauldhouse

Travel To Space

T ravelling felt like death
R unning around to fix the ship
A t Mars, it was peaceful
V oodoos were everywhere
E vening came, the light went out
L eaving Mars to Milky Way.

T ime flew past
O n Mars, peace left.

S tarting to light
P eople awake
A s if by magic, lights go off
C oming down the stairs
E ating lunch on my chair.

Max Macfarlane (11)
Falla Hill Primary School, Fauldhouse

Sugar Candy Extravaganza

The cloud was running and he fell
Deep, deep down into a dark well
Bumped his head on the way down
And now he's left with an unfortunate frown.

Now he's on sugar rush
Soft and sound on his way to Lush
Sound asleep then he heard a cotton car beep
When he was asleep, he was counting sheep.

He found a nickle
When he was eating pickles
I went zooming through the sky
It felt like I was about to fly.

Lauren McMillan (10)
Falla Hill Primary School, Fauldhouse

Haribo Mayhem

Have you ever seen a Haribo?
A Haribo so large
A Haribo so big
As big as a barge
Well if you have, I bet you have never ever seen
A Haribo bigger than me.

I'm much bigger than a lion's paw
I'm very ginormous and kind
You can see me from far away
I'm not that hard to find
I'm very green
And smile all the time
Because being happy means you can
Laugh, have fun and play.

Caitlin Donnelly (11)
Falla Hill Primary School, Fauldhouse

Candy Land

C andy, yum! *Crack!* As I opened the jar,

A rghhhh! As I choked on a sweet

N ooooo! As I dropped the sweets on the floor

D is for chocolate dip

Y ay! As I get my favourite sweet

L is for lollipop

A rghhhh! As I went through the candy in alphabetical order

N oooo! As I slipped on the banana

D is for a sour dummy.

Cameron Mullen (9)

Falla Hill Primary School, Fauldhouse

Black Hole Steak

I woke up on the moon and found a steak on the ground
I went out to take a look, got covered in some gloop
Then covered in some poop, I got the steak!
The steak was mind-blowing, Granny Granny!
The steak was slowing
Granny tried the steak, she passed out
Grampa was bound to be back
A black hole appeared and Grampa came back
Grampa, why? I'm the Devil.

Mark Reilly (10)
Falla Hill Primary School, Fauldhouse

The Burger That Came From Space

The giant thing came from space
We didn't know what it was
Then we called for help
A siren went off which was loud
We tried to evacuate
But we couldn't
The burger was already super close
An hour later, it crashed into
A 500-storey building.

I bailed out of the city
Then two days later,
I came back and saw the hole.

James Walker (9)
Falla Hill Primary School, Fauldhouse

Swimming In Lava

S aturdays are for swimming in lava
W ow
I n volcanoes, ducks swim in lava
M ermaids and ducks both swim in lava
M ostly, mermaids swim in lava
I really like to swim in lava
N o one can swim in lava because it is dangerous
G race, my sister, would love to swim in lava.

Kirsten Law (10)
Falla Hill Primary School, Fauldhouse

Opposite Land

This magical land of opposite
Where boys are girls, do you get it?
With a chocolate ocean
And popping candy sand
Oh, what an amazing Opposite Land!

This magical land of opposite
With many marshmallow trees
I took a little nibble
And all I could taste was
The little pit of sand.

Chloe Cunningham (10)
Falla Hill Primary School, Fauldhouse

Skiing Panda

The panda stands on the snowy hill
But Panda is scared because
He has to ski downhill - oh no!
Panda is careful to not fall
He starts to ski slow - oh no!
He is speeding fast, arghhhh!
He does not fall in the snow
Oh yeah!

Leona Lawrence (11)
Falla Hill Primary School, Fauldhouse

Living Objects

The day objects came to life was a disaster
My bed was bopping up and down
My clothes tried to hide from me
My pencil said the words instead of writing them
All my clothes were on my bed when I got home.

Riley Burns (9)
Falla Hill Primary School, Fauldhouse

The Volcano

L ava pours from the volcano
A nd gets thrown out the top
V ultures circle the volcano
A s blackbirds follow.

Kelsey Mcdougall (10)
Falla Hill Primary School, Fauldhouse

Underwater Houses

I was swimming around in the deep ocean blue
When I found an abandoned little street
What I saw was very strange
Houses floating everywhere I looked.

Houses that weren't floating were tied down by vines
Some were very small as if they were for a mouse
Others were very large as if they were for a whale!
This was all strange, very strange indeed!

There was nothing to hear in this place of misery,
Only the swish of the waves from above,
I opened my mouth in shock but instead of fresh air
I got a mouthful of saltwater.

I swam to the houses that were held down,
To my surprise, I felt the wall, it turned to dust
As I returned to the surface, I was thinking
Where did those houses come from?

Samantha Murray (11)
High Mill Primary School, Carluke

The Dancing UFO Unicorns

If you have extra quadruple eyesight,
You'll see the dancing UFO unicorns and ice creams
Blasting cold creams down to the Earth
The unicorns blasting laser beams out of their UFOs.
If you have amazing times ten hearing
You can hear music blaring out of the UFO
You'll also hear the unicorns' mushrooms saying, "Moo!"
If you can smell really brilliantly times fifteen,
You can smell the unicorns' fresh candy
Scent of candyfloss and the UFO gas
If you can feel really good
You'll feel the ice cream's cold cream blast
If you can taste super spectacularly
You will taste the fresh ice cream flakes
Floating in the air.

Matthew Russell (10)
High Mill Primary School, Carluke

Dancing Ice Cream On A Cloud

I see a dancing ice cream on a cloud going to
space
I hear the sound of music going away from Earth
I see the dancing ice cream waving at me
So I follow it up to space.

I see a bear driving a flying car, I jump on.
The bear takes me up to space
I see the ice cream on the cloud, still dancing
I got closer then I jump on the cloud
I see the bear go away, back to Earth
I take the dancing ice cream down to Earth.

I see the cloud land on the grass so I get off
I see the dancing ice cream go back up to space,
oh no!

Sarah Madill (9)
High Mill Primary School, Carluke

Elves In Space

Existing adventures all around the galaxy
Lots of stars glittering and glowing all through the
galaxy
Full of elves, not any humans in sight
Saturn glowing and lighting up the galaxy.
I see all the floating elves bobbing up and down
Never-ending galaxy full of stars and planets.
Space will never be normal, it is Space Land
People puzzled where the elves had gone
Asteroids shooting by heading straight for Earth
Can the elves watch this happen to Earth?
Elves never leave space.

Jasmin Peebles (10)
High Mill Primary School, Carluke

Wizard Hippopotamus On Hoverboards

Flying in the sky, casting lots of spells,
Turning people into water wells
Blue in colour, loud in sound
To fly his hoverboard costs a billion pounds
It roars and casts more, looking for fights,
For it thinks it has extreme might.
Making more mops fly, it was more mad
Then it made everything on Earth ironclad
It fell to the ground, then opened a door
And it drank water once more.

Oliver Isik (10)
High Mill Primary School, Carluke

Jelly Burger

Once there was a jelly burger
There was a rainbow cloud
There was a wonderful smell
Where was it coming from?
It was coming from everywhere
It was coming from cheese
Salad and lavender
I hear Jelly Burger screaming
The rainbow went away then it came back
It was getting brighter and brighter
Then all my food came out.

Dominic Dickson (10)
High Mill Primary School, Carluke

Flying Dogs

F lying dogs in the sky
L ooking up in the light blue sky
Y ellow, golden and bright sunlight
I see them flying in the sky
N ight-time will be coming soon
G oing to go away tonight.

D ogs flying fastly
O vernight, they drift away
G oing to come back one day.

Chelsea Gault (11)
High Mill Primary School, Carluke

Candy World

C andy, it's so, so sweet and sugary to eat

A nd you must come over here and see this
amazing world of sweet, sweet candy

N ever shall I leave such a wonderful place

D ay after day, I eat the sweet, sweet candy but
also I eat some healthy fruit as well

Y es, I know it is unhealthy but I do eat fruit as
well, at least I'm being healthy sometimes.

W elcome to my home, filled with a lifetime supply
of sweet, sweet candy but remember to eat
healthy fruit as well

O r you might end up with no teeth at all

R un along and play happily before I call you in
for supper

L ast day here so get in, it's time to go home

D ay after day, we go down to Earth to buy
healthy food to eat as well as unhealthy so bye
for now.

Bethany Louise Fenwick (9)
Riverbank School, Aberdeen

The Ice Cream Planet

On a sunny day,
I see the news, what does it say?
There is a planet made out of ice cream
Oh, that will be a wonderful dream
How, oh how can I get there?
When I get to school, guess what I will share?
Then I bring my box of Lego
Build a rocket ship, I am a pro
I am flying into space
I hope the planet is a wonderful place
What is that colourful, spiky sphere?
Maybe the planet doesn't want me to get there
How can I escape the spikes?
I need to get to my wonderful likes
Then I build a Lego laser gun
Laser the spikes off, now let's have some fun
I am in the ice cream planet
Hey, there is an ice cream, let's eat it
What are those ice cream aliens?

Time to get back into my rocket ship
Oh, what a great time
Why did I leave the world of shine?

Joshua Ufiegbe (8)
Riverbank School, Aberdeen

Halloween

H ey my name is Sophie

A KA the girl that's won the Halloween competition for the last five years

L ast year, I got free drinks because I won for the last four years

L ife is awesome when people call me the Halloween Queen

O utside, people kept bullying me because they didn't think I deserved to be the Halloween Queen

W hile that was happening, the disco was ending

E veryone was very tired, I managed to get away from the bullies

E veryone was quiet when I walked into the disco room, they all stared at me

N ever be the Halloween Queen!

Sophie Brown (8)
Riverbank School, Aberdeen

The Cheese Boy

T om likes cheese

H e also loves blue cheese

E specially, he likes soy cheese.

C ares about mozzarella cheese

H e just loves cheese

E specially the yummy, white, soft cheese, he loves it

E ats cheese every day for breakfast

S mells cheese with his giant nose

E ats lunch with fries and big fat chunks of cheese on top.

B ig fat blobs of cheese for a snack

O h no, he is a greedy, big cheese monster

Y ou can't stop me eating cheese.

Maja Anna Kertesz (8)

Riverbank School, Aberdeen

The Day The Sun Exploded!

I woke up feeling hot
I checked if my flower was still in the pot
"Hey Flower, are you there?"
I leaned over and the flower was all dried out
I looked out of the window
And saw the sun bigger and fatter
"That's why it was so super hot!"
And the sun exploded with lava
But I was lucky, I had a giant pool
Of freezing cold water
I jumped in it and lived happily ever after
Before the end, I was fur and heard a purr
And it was an adorable kitten, I took it home.

Nikola Joanna Ojrzynska (9)
Riverbank School, Aberdeen

Halloween

H alloween is really spooky

A ll the kids are going to the school disco

L ovely lights, lovely lights, oh what lovely lights

L onely pumpkins, lonely pumpkins, awww poor pumpkins

O nly black cats give you good luck

W hen it's Halloween, we get pumpkins

E verybody can dress up for Halloween

E verything is better when it's Halloween

N obody is too old to go trick or treating.

Lilly Youngson (9)

Riverbank School, Aberdeen

The Flying Hamster

One day, there was a hamster
The hamster was a gangster
His name was Tim
He liked to swim
He liked to win
The hamster liked to draw
He liked to chew on straw
He thought he had paws
He liked beef that was raw
He had tiny claws
The hamster could fly
He saw people cry
He flew up to Unicorn Land
Which was made out of sand
When he saw people cry, he flew up high
After that, Tim said bye.

Majka Nicole Dzieza (9)
Riverbank School, Aberdeen

Grumpy Cat

G rumpy cats are annoying

R eally cruel

U nder the bed you hear him purring

M any people hate him

P eople give him dog food

Y ou will be scared of him because he's mean.

C ross your fingers and toes so he doesn't scratch

A ndy, his dad, loves him because he isn't grumpy to him

T wo people are nice to him so he is nice to the people.

Holly Robertson (8)
Riverbank School, Aberdeen

Super Slime

S erious Man was here, don't you fear
U niversity time, see ya children
P ink slime, fluffy slime
E lectricity had gone because of fluffy slime
R azor slime, white speckles.

S quishy slime, go go slime
L ike my new football boots
I 'm not wanting slimy hair
M ash'ems watery inside but not outside
E veryone likes slime.

Kenzie Innes (9)
Riverbank School, Aberdeen

Crocodile

C rocodiles don't chomp, they stomp
R otten meat they eat
O pen your eyes and see the danger
C rocs and crocodiles are siblings
O ver probably 100 different crocodiles
D ucks are one of the many things they eat
I have seen a crocodile, a big one
L ost in the forest
E veryone watch out, crocodiles can fly.

Cally Hannah MacDonald (9)

Riverbank School, Aberdeen

The Crazy Shop

One day, I walked into a shop
I saw an enormous mop
There even was a crazy cat
And I'm pretty sure his name was Pat
And the cat kept on scratching me so I said stop
And then I heard a quiet noise,
Which was made by a tortoise
Then I saw something weird
The tortoise had a big beard...
So I decided to exit the crazy shop!

Adam Tomczakowski (9)
Riverbank School, Aberdeen

The Rainbow Cotton Candy Cloud

I was floating on a rainbow cotton candy cloud but
suddenly...
It began to rain
The cloud got all sticky and wet
I got stuck
"Oh, why did I want to float on a cloud?"
The cloud disappeared
I was falling
Then I landed on flowers.

Charley Laing (9)
Riverbank School, Aberdeen

The Crazy Unicorn

There was a unicorn that didn't have teeth
And he lived underneath a green leaf
And he didn't have teeth because he didn't like meat
Because it smells like feet.
But the unicorn was sweet
And he lived on my street.

Maja Swiderska (9)
Riverbank School, Aberdeen

The Briefcase Chase

A girl called Grace
Was on a briefcase chase!
The case had a face that you can't trace
It had no waist, it was silver-laced
The case that could race outran her pace.

Kayla-Marie O'Driscoll (9)
Riverbank School, Aberdeen

If I Was A Wizard

If I was a wizard,
I would cast some spells,
A lot of things would happen,
There might be funny smells!

I could turn you into a ferret,
And bounce you round and round,
The air would fill with vapour and mist
You feet would leave the ground!

I'd say lots of magic things
Like 'Accio' or 'Stinging Hex'
It would all be very fast
No idea what would happen next!

I'd mix up lots of potions,
Made with 'truth serum' or 'polyjuice'
I'd offer it to you to drink
Or mix it in a mousse.

Maybe I'll come to school one day
In a cloak and with a wand

I'd cast a special teacher spell
And turn you into a frog in a pond!

Bo Cox (7)
Royal Blind School, Edinburgh

Apples, Oranges And Bananas

I like apples, they are very sweet
I like oranges, they're a favourite treat!
I don't like bananas, because they are too soft
When I try to eat them, I feel like I will cough!

I like apples, they are nice and red
I like oranges, I'd even eat one in my bed!
I don't like bananas, they make me feel quite sick
If I was given one, I'd get rid of it real quick!

I like apples, I eat one every day
I like oranges - hooray! Hooray!
I don't like bananas, but I sometimes wish I did
Maybe I will try again, after all I'm just a kid!

Rebeka Ritchie (11)
Royal Blind School, Edinburgh

What's It Like In A Drop Of Water?

I fell into the sea, oh yes I did
Everyone climbed into their own drops of water
I saw whale sharks swimming around eating
plantation
The whales were colossal
The swordfish had an extremely sharp sword
The wind picked us up to rain
When we were up in the sky, I saw a dragon
It was sleeping in the clouds,
Oh the way he was sleeping, he almost fell
When I finally fell down
It was the most beautiful thing I ever saw
There were multicoloured dwarves roaming the
streets
Purple goblins working for money,
I also saw all my family and friends
(In a drop of water as well)
I hit the sand where I was playing
Everyone shouted, "Don't go in the water, Bob!"

Archie Donaldson (9)
St Leonards School, The Pends

Candy Chaos

The snow was of outrageous height
I don't know what happened that night
I sank through the snow
I don't know how low
But it gave me a massive fright.

I landed in a magical land
With lots of candy in my hand
I could smell the fresh flowers wrapped in a band
And deep in the sand
Wrapped in a band
There was a letter made out of sweets from Candy
Land
and
In that letter it said...
You have got fifty minutes each season
Find the end of the rainbow and you will be free
from Candy Land!

That minute the land began to shake and
Suddenly autumn was awake!

I saw the leaves scattered on the ground
It made a lovely rustling sound
But back to the colourful rainbow
I saw it in the distance
I ran up to it and
I was home! Woohoo!

Lana McGuire (9)
St Leonards School, The Pends

School Is The Worst

School is the worst, it is just so bad
The teacher is always so mean, angry and mad
I want something exciting and fun
Like burn the teacher in the sun.
School is the worst, it is just so boring
The headmaster is old and is always snoring.
I want something exciting and happy
Like annoy the headmaster's wife, Miss Mary.
School is the worst, it is just so hard
The deputy head is as thin as a card.
I want something exciting and happy
Like throwing the deputy's head in a nappy.
School is the worst but I like my friends
and at least school isn't on at the weekends!

Emily Rose Anderson (8)
St Leonards School, The Pends

What's Down A Cliff?

Wouldn't you agree tying your shoelaces is
annoying?
Especially when they are wet and damp
They stick to this and stick to that
And because of that, I fell down flat
And rolled off the edge of a cliff.

You wouldn't believe it if I told you
But a huge, green cabbage with wings
And a carrot unicorn horn
And a cucumber elephant trunk picked me up.

The thing that spooked me most
Was when it forced me to eat his cabbage-green
gum
The gum was sticky
The gum was icky
And I spat it out immediately.

Conor MacKay (9)
St Leonards School, The Pends

Trouble With Lion Teeth

I polish lions' teeth
I put my hand underneath
Yuck, that crisp meat
I can see yellow crumbling teeth
I can hear grunts and moans
And for a treat, I give it an ice cream cone
I stick my head in and see
Swelling gums and it's a garbage dump unlike me
I feel saliva on me
It's sticky and gooey, yuck!
I see it's getting dark and
I see the mouth close shut
Help me!

Willow Manifold (10)
St Leonards School, The Pends

Og The Ogre

Og was an ogre, he lived with his family
Og loved Coke and his family
Loved fires and fires bring smoke
Every night, they go off for a fight
Mille, Gambal and Mike
But as all of them go off for their fight
Og stays at home with sheer delight
Then one day he got told by his parents
To go and fight
But what did he do?
I don't know, I don't know.

Verity Swift (9)
St Leonards School, The Pends

Thunderstorm

Thunderstorms so truly horrendous
Really?
Just kidding, I think they're tremendous
Lighting also shining so bright
Just like the stars on a cold winter's night
Thunder as well as it starts to roar
I feel as strong and as fast as a boar
As the skies start to clear
I feel sad and a tear
But then I remind myself
It will come back this year.

Cameron Duncan (9)
St Leonards School, The Pends

Over The Rainbow

Over the rainbow, what do you find?
A huge pot of gold in some people's mind
But no, that's not true
All you would find is a big, big portal to
somebody's loo
I look out of the loo, what do I see?
A land of fairies looking at me
Pixies and elves, goblins too
What did I do? It's only a loo.

Ben Alexander Smeddle (8)
St Leonards School, The Pends

The Sloth With Beaver Teeth

I saw a sloth with beaver teeth
Cutting down a tree.
Then he chewed it into chip bark,
He threw the chip bark in the river
And waited for a long time
For fish to eat the chip bark.
So he tried to eat the chip bark
To see if it worked
And he choked to death.

Lewis Hanton (9)
St Leonards School, The Pends

Lego City

There's a happy Lego City
Smart cars driving busily
I love to watch them on Christmas Eve.
There's a happy Lego City
Buses zooming past
Until I see the last.
There's a happy Lego City
With mini figures walking free
I wish one of them was me.

Jonny Chernin (8)
St Leonards School, The Pends

Untitled

Bananas, bananas
They are yellow
Bananas, bananas
They are green
You can get black bananas
They are mean
They are squidgy and squeaky
They annoy me
I would rather have them green.

Aidan Jon MacKay (7)
St Leonards School, The Pends

The Bananas Come To Life

Dad spotted a banana
Then a head popped up and legs too
A banana man, who knew
It started to run for its life
If you see one I would run
They have armies that come after you.

Julius Gill (8)
St Leonards School, The Pends

My Bananas

(Haiku poetry)

I don't like them black
Bananas are better green
They are too squashy

Green bananas hard
I like green bananas best
I don't eat the rest.

Francis Maughan (8)
St Leonards School, The Pends

Fast Food

I love burgers
Because they don't have legs
We are lucky
Sometimes you get the odd one with legs
They run very fast
When you eat them.

Theo Gautreau (7)
St Leonards School, The Pends

My Banana

My banana is yummy
After it explodes
It's black
It's not yummy
It's burnt.

Simon Schwoebel (8)
St Leonards School, The Pends

Monkey Gymnastics

Helly, my name is Emily Hut
I have a monkey that can do tricks like a gymnast
like me
My monkey has big strong muscles...
But one day my pet fell down
She had a very bad cut that made her cry all day
long
But one day we sent her to a good wizard
The wizard made her happy
He made her as happy as a hippopotamus
Monkey carefully skipped home while I ran home
As soon as we got home Monkey started to do
gymnastics.

Ayomide Olawuyi (9)
St Roch's RC Primary School, Glasgow

Crazy Space

I went to space to tie my lace
I found out that it was amazing because I saw the sun
The sun was as hot as fire
Then something crazy happened!
I met a friendly dinosaur, he could talk and he let me ride him
There was fruit that had faces with suitcases
I saw all big planets
I wasn't wearing a spacesuit but I never died
Then I ate the moon until I was full.
After, I went back to Earth but no one was there.

Sonia Kester (9)
St Roch's RC Primary School, Glasgow

Underpant World Bumps Into Unicorn World

The Unicorn World is magical and beautiful
This is why
They're colourful
Here are the colours purple, pink and blue,
They have glitter on them too
Here is Underpants World,
He doesn't like Unicorn World because
She is beautiful, perfect and colourful so
He is so jealous, then one day he was so mad
He bumped into Unicorn World
She got hurt and she was mad.

Cara Trainer (9)
St Roch's RC Primary School, Glasgow

Burgers Falling From The Sky

Burgers falling from the sky and waking me up
Hamburgers so big and juicy
Made me want to eat them quickly
Yum, yum, yum
So I went out to eat it all up
Yum, yum, yum
Then a bunch of hamburgers were falling down
When a bunch of hamburgers were falling, I ate them
Hamburgers come in all sizes
Some small and some the size of a house.

Javaid Naqvi (8)
St Roch's RC Primary School, Glasgow

Flying In The Sky

Flying in the sky so fun, scary and very fun
But be careful you might hit something... *Bang!*... It
will be very sore
People will say, "Wow, that person is flying, it's very
nice!"
I flew to school, I hit a bunch of birds, it was very
unsafe
In school I could not control myself
So I flew out of school and it was no good.

Ryan Liu (8)
St Roch's RC Primary School, Glasgow

Arshad The King And Ally McClare

Arshad is lonely sitting in the dark of night
Ally the candy sitting in the sparks of light
Arshad is so insane sitting in the frame
But it was his only choice for it to not be so lame
Arshad was gliding on the dinosaur that day
Then he said, "Oh, I will never pay."
Ally said, "That is not okay."

Arshad Mughery (9)
St Roch's RC Primary School, Glasgow

Eating The Earth

When I ate the Earth
It turned black and white
Then dark was the only weather forever and ever
When the Earth got eaten
Everybody was angry
I wanted to give back the Earth
But I liked it very much
The Earth was the same shape as a big football
So when I ate the Earth
I was sorry and put it back.

Victor Akintula (9)

St Roch's RC Primary School, Glasgow

The Crazy Dinosaur

We saw a dinosaur in the playground
The crazy brontosaurus running all over the big playground
The brontosaurus eats the leaves on the smallest tree
The children climb on the brontosaurus
Like climbing up the highest mountain in the country
Laughing, laughing, laughing loudly, shouting loudly too.

Yu Fan Li (9)
St Roch's RC Primary School, Glasgow

Funny Actions!

Running in the air and walking in the sea to Asia
Jumping to the sun and dancing on lava is so fun
Licking a shark on a rocket ship all the way to
Mercury
Learning to speak Alien on Mars, Mercury and
Saturn.
Eating fire and drinking lava is so fun
Raid is screaming and the Earth is jumping.

Shabib Khan (8)
St Roch's RC Primary School, Glasgow

Licking A Whale

I saw a whale eating a snail and it had a smile
I saw a whale, it had a smile
The whale was splashing the water
Splash, splash, splash
The whale was hitting and I hit him back
The whale was so angry because he was lonely
The whale was so happy because he went to a party.

Natnael Tekle (9)
St Roch's RC Primary School, Glasgow

Playing With God

One day I flew to Heaven
And a lovely angel took me to God
God was doing silly dances
On a fluffy cloud.
When God saw me he said,
"Callum, do you want to play tag?" and
I said, "Yes."

Callum McDermid (9)
St Roch's RC Primary School, Glasgow

Blow Bubbles Into Moon Craters

I was on the moon
Blowing bubbles into moon craters
The bubbles popped
I flew away
I will go back to the moon.

Andy Chen (9)
St Roch's RC Primary School, Glasgow

Giant Space Monster

G rantie was his name.

I was so afraid when I saw him.

A nd no one was with me, just me and Grantie.

N ever come to Mars, ever!

T his is super scary. I'm panicking!

S o I had to run away.

P lease help me, please!

A t the base I think no one is there.

C ome please, my oxygen is running out!

E van, my friend, please get your suit and come here

M an alive, he can fly, please come quick.

O h my, actually Grantie is a robot controlled by aliens.

N o! He's got a laser and I've just got a net.

S wish! My net actually worked. It took off the laser.

T here's Evan with a laser.

E van shot the laser and finished Grantie off.

R ight then I farted because I had beans for breakfast!

Logan Iain Anderson (9)
Strathpeffer Primary School, Strathpeffer

My Head Teacher Is A Dragon

D ragons?
R eally, are you sure?
A pparently my head teacher is one too
G reat, she even breathes fire
O h no, I better run
N o, please don't burn our work!

H opefully everyone is lying
E veryone has seen
A figure breathing fire
D on't you dare move

T hat is if you don't want to be burnt
E ach and every day she hides in her office
A nother day goes by and I think I should see her
with my own eyes
C ome on, I have to see her to know that it is true
H elp, aaaaah! It is true
E ventually I got over my fear
R ight, is everything back to normal now?

Laura MacDonald (10)
Strathpeffer Primary School, Strathpeffer

Animals Speaking English

A nimals speaking?

N o, that's rubbish

I don't believe it! You're lying!

M ike the dinosaur spoke English!

A nimals... speaking... English?

L ook, it's Larry the lion!

"S ay, am I annoying? Of course I'm not! Ha ha!"

S orry, you're right and... aah, a lion!

P retty annoying Larry is...

E ven Larry has a girlfriend called Liz!

A h... she's so pretty... she drives a Lamborghini!

K eep putting earplugs in!

I don't like Ali the Anteater either...

N ever did I imagine animals speak English!

G oodness, please please don't...

Heed my warning, heed!

Eilidh Scott (10)
Strathpeffer Primary School, Strathpeffer

Living In A Cupcake

L iving in a cupcake is very strange.
I have a dog made out of sweets.
V ery soft icing my bed is on the icing.
I n the cupcake smells so good.
N ever eat the cupcake because I live there.
G ooey icing is on the top of the cupcake.

I n the cupcake I have a TV.
N atie my dog eats all the food.

A cupcake is very cool.

C upcakes are very colourful.
U sually I love living in a cupcake.
P laying is very fun in the Cupcake.
C upcakes are very tasty.
A s tasty as can be.
K atie is my friend, she lives with me.
E ilidh lives with me as well.

Living in a cupcake!

Jessica Emily Cameron (10)
Strathpeffer Primary School, Strathpeffer

Living In A Zoo

I woke up in the flamingo's bed.
But ouch, something was pecking at my head!
"Scare them away!" the monkey king shouts,
"Come up to my tree house and have some
Brussels sprouts."
"No thanks," I said
But he shouted, "Come up here now!"
I wanted to get out but I didn't know how.
Suddenly, I was off the ground
With one enormous bound.
Luckily, I managed to escape
And found myself a fancy cape.
I felt powerful and brave
Never mind, I fell in a cave.
I was screaming, "Help!"
And a bear cub began to yelp.
Mamma bear was angry and was ready for tea
Please oh please, don't eat me!

Sophie Kay (10)
Strathpeffer Primary School, Strathpeffer

The Alien Who Wouldn't Speak!

One day, I went to outer space
And then I saw a bright green face.
I took him back to my house
My mum thought he was a mouse.
The next day, I took him to my school
I took him in the swimming pool.
Yes, the pool, that's what I said
Suddenly, he had a carrot head.
I spoke, I yapped, I talked to him
I just realised he was an alien.
Later on, we went to bed
"I'm going home," he finally said!
Just that night, I followed him back
The aliens threw me into a sack.
They ice skated on the moon
My mum shouted for me at noon.
But they captured me forever and ever
I wanted to go home but they didn't let me, never.

Sarah Amaya Decarole Butler-Whittaker (10)

Strathpeffer Primary School, Strathpeffer

My Brother Came From A Meteor

My brother came from a meteor, that is a fact.
I thought it was just a silly act.
My mum told me to be very, very proud
And not to tell the rest of the crowd.
One day, I went to my new school.
Then we went to the swimming pool.
All my friends just found out
My brother's head was a Brussels sprout.
They all started to scream and shout!
Very quickly I had to swim out.
When I got home, I found my dad
Looking very sad.
It all blew over very fast
I think it will be the last
Of the boy who has a veggie head!

Hew Rasdale (10)
Strathpeffer Primary School, Strathpeffer

A Man From The Land Of Sweets

The most peculiar man
Went by in a sweetie van
A liquorice moustache
But he had no cash
Lollipop eyes and a top hat made of pies
His hands were made of sweet rock candy
Very handy if you want some candy
His trousers were made of lovely whipped cream
It feels so much like a dream
His hair was pink candyfloss
He would soon have hair loss
His scarf was a rainbow strip
And he had one big chewy lip
His coat was made of liquorice
It was absolutely delish
Oh no, here come the kids
The sweet man has no chance
But then he began to dance

Then he vanished
He was banished
He's away from our land
Oh, this tale was grand!

Freya Waite (9)
Strathpeffer Primary School, Strathpeffer

The Tasty Pear

Once, there was a pear,
Waiting in the fresh air.
He was a beautiful pear,
He also had brown hair.
He was small and round,
And also weighed a hundred pound.
We decided to have a BBQ,
But before we even touched him, he split in two!
When he was ready,
He was messing with my head, eek!
Once I was done,
I probably weighed a ton.
When it got dark,
We had to leave the park.

James MacGillivray (10)
Strathpeffer Primary School, Strathpeffer

The Sea Is Yellow And The Sun Is Blue!

One day, I went to the seaside
The sea was yellow and the sun was blue
Then I saw a kangaroo
The kangaroo went into the water
It was getting hotter
It was as hot
As a stew pot
But then my mum bought a crisp bag
But then I realised my jumper still had the tag
The sea is yellow and the sun is blue
Maybe it's my imagination
I don't know
I should put on a show
About the difference of them
But maybe I will just write an anthem.

Katie Jankowski (10)
Strathpeffer Primary School, Strathpeffer

The Nessie King

T he Nessie is the king
H e is big and blue
E ating like a monster

N essie lives under a bed
E ating fish all the time
S noring like a bear
S limy like a slug if you see him
I s he sleeping?
E rm, he is... the Nessie

K ing of the sea!
I can hear him from here
N osy like a nose
G ross like a bogey. Yuck!

Brooke Mackenzie (10)
Strathpeffer Primary School, Strathpeffer

Sally's Secret School Bag

Super Sally went to school
She thought that all kids rule

Suddenly, Sally shrunk
Fell in her school bag and saw a skunk!

She wandered around
With a fox and hound

The fox had a box
And the hound had an ox

She went further in
And saw a bin

Sally could feel herself starting to grow
Then she shouted, "Woah!"

Now she takes a great big step out
Then Sally looks about...

Ruby Frame (10)
Strathpeffer Primary School, Strathpeffer

Flying Too High

Once, I met a powerful witch
She was standing on a pitch
She gave me a spell that made me fly
But suddenly, I went too high
Why oh why did I want to fly?
Suddenly, I began to cry
Oh look, there's a guy
Oh thank you, I began to cry
And as I began to float down
I saw the king wearing a crown
I said when I got down from the sky
I'm never again in my life going to fly!

Keira Syrjanen (10)
Strathpeffer Primary School, Strathpeffer

So High In The Sky

I like to sit on a cloud eating seagulls, it makes me proud
The seagulls can be very loud
The seagull's heart
Tastes like strawberry tart
His feathers are fluffy
So he is very puffy
His beak is like a pair of pliers
But seagulls can be little liars
Its eyes are crunchy, as crunchy as a Dorito
They go down well with a sip of mojito!

Finlee Irvine (9)
Strathpeffer Primary School, Strathpeffer

Burger

B urger beauty brightens your eyes,

U nderground are unusual ugly things that have not been uncovered,

R un, run round the ring but beware of the ketchup sauce,

G reen gherkins everybody hates,

E at everything, even the ketchup ring,

R elish is running round every night!

Ellie-Rose Scott (10)

Strathpeffer Primary School, Strathpeffer

Bouncing On A Cupcake

When I was bouncing on some cupcakes I saw
some sweets,
With the sweets, I saw some treats.
The cupcakes taste so sweet,
Then I saw someone's feet.
The feet were red,
"Just like a cherry," I said.
They were so big,
Just like an oil rig.
They were so frilly,
I thought they were so silly!

Connie Mackain (10)
Strathpeffer Primary School, Strathpeffer

YOUNG WRITERS INFORMATION

We hope you have enjoyed reading this book – and that you will continue to in the coming years.

If you're a young writer who enjoys reading and creative writing, or the parent of an enthusiastic poet or story writer, do visit our website **www.youngwriters.co.uk**. Here you will find free competitions, workshops and games, as well as recommended reads, a poetry glossary and our blog. There's lots to keep budding writers motivated to write!

If you would like to order further copies of this book, or any of our other titles, then please give us a call or visit **www.youngwriters.co.uk**.

Young Writers
Remus House
Coltsfoot Drive
Peterborough
PE2 9BF
(01733) 890066
info@youngwriters.co.uk

Join in the conversation!
Tips, news, giveaways and much more!

 YoungWritersUK    @YoungWritersCW